MABEL
and the Fire

WRITTEN BY ALISON HINSON ILLUSTRATED BY ERIN TAYLOR

Text © Alison Hinson 2020
Visit www.ErinTaylorIllustrator.com

When reading this book with children please keep the following in mind:

Natural disasters and other personal experiences of tragedy can be extremely difficult for children as they do best with predictability, structure, and security. Adults and children respond differently to tragedies and trauma. While adults are able to understand events with more logical and rational thinking, children's understanding of events is not always as well-developed. When children experience catastrophic events, whether personally or through someone close to them, children may show behaviors to display their fear and anxiety that might seem extreme to adults. While the majority of these reactions are normal, without proper support and reassurance from caregiving adults, the impact of these events can stay with children for a long time or develop into more intensive emotional and behavioral symptoms. The following information can assist you in using this book to help your child express their experience and help you to understand your child's fears and concerns. By supporting children through difficult experiences we can help them become resilient and grow stronger through experience.

Express your love in a variety of ways-
Tell your children you love them more than you usually do, through your words and physically with lots of hugs, even if your child doesn't show outward signs of distress. Reading together and giving positive touch can help restore a child's sense of safety and security. Foster a sense of connection by staying close if possible and if you must leave, prepare your child with advanced notice so that you have time to address feelings, provide assurances they will be safe, and that you will be back. Be there for your children as much as possible when they need to talk about the disaster.

Maintain normal routines as much as possible-
Predictable events and schedules are reassuring during times of stress for children. Keeping a consistent sense of security and routine is one of the most important things you can provide for your children who find comfort and safety in the routines and structure of their everyday lives. Encourage your child to participate in normal activities and keep the family routine as much as possible.

Keep bedtime calm-
if you are reading this story at bedtime you will need to allow more time than usual for this transition, if needed. Reading the story before bedtime may create challenges to the child's ability to sleep or increase the possibility of nightmares so it is recommended that the story be used during the day with plenty of time for adult attention and time for listening and talking through your child's feelings.

Provide children with opportunities to express their thoughts and feelings-
Remember that of all the things children/people need in times of crisis, the most important is the chance to talk about their reactions and experiences. Focus on your children's feelings and thoughts and take your lead from them in terms of what they

need and what they are thinking and feeling. Do this without judgment or suggestions; it is ok to discuss how your child's feelings are the same or different to those of the characters in the story. Point out facial expressions, and help the child to "wonder" about what the characters are thinking and feeling as a way of understanding how your child may have experienced the event. Allow anxieties to surface by letting your child know it is normal to feel worried or upset. Do not minimize your child's fears and concerns. It is okay if your child gets upset. When they talk about scary or disturbing things, you can then reassure them and help them to feel safe and secure. Supply words if your child has difficulty labeling how they feel. Share your own reactions in moderation and without overwhelming your children with your feelings. Let them know that you share some of their concerns. It is up to parents to interpret what has happened. Provide facts, in line with your child's age and level of understanding. Keep your answers to your children's questions simple and age-appropriate. They may visit their concerns briefly and then turn to play or do schoolwork. This is a way that children can avoid feeling overwhelmed or too scared. Look for signs of increased anxiety in your children, remembering that each one may communicate upset feelings in different ways. Seek additional professional help if you see ongoing and/or significant physical symptoms such as stomach aches or headaches or any behavioral changes such as unusual hyperactivity, drops in grades, not wanting to go to school, excessive crying, withdrawal, increased clinginess, loss of interest in their usual activities, or lack of their usual enjoyment in life.

Children are influenced by their parents' reactions.

Children carefully watch parents to see how they should react to serious events. Children look to their parents to determine how worried they should be and often adopt the same feelings and behaviors as their parents. When you get your needs met, then you can be available to care for your children's needs. Try to find other adults to talk about your feelings so as not to burden or overwhelm your children. It is important to do your best to try to bring a sense of control and hope for your child. It's okay if you don't know exactly what to say; sometimes there is no answer that will make everything okay. However, doing your best to tell your child that they are loved and safe will help them to understand and cope.

Reassure your child that your family and community are safe.

Let your child know that you will protect them, and that events like this are rare. Children may not want to talk for long periods of time about the trauma. If your child seems reluctant to talk, but you believe they are upset, you can help by being calm, loving, and reassuring- do not try to force your child to talk. Instead, allow your child to express themselves through less intense options such as drawing or playing out feelings and experiences. Tell them that there will always be someone there to protect and take care of them.

Mabel was a very *happy* dog. She had a nice home, a boy who *loved* her, and her favorite chew toy that she played with every day.

One day it began to get very smoky outside. It was so smoky that Mabel and her boy could not play outside. It was hot, and stinky, and very **boring**.

Mabel's family said it was smoky because there was a fire nearby. The smoke got thicker and thicker. Mabel's family began to get **worried**. Mabel's family said they might need to leave their house so they could stay **safe**.

Mabel hoped the fire would not come closer to the house, but it did. Mabel's family packed up the clothes and toys that would fit into the car. They had to hurry. Mabel felt very **sad** and **confused** about leaving her house and toys behind.

The family drove to their grandmother's house to stay while they decided what to do next.

They could only stay for a little while because the house was too **crowded** for Mabel and her whole family.

Mabel's family had to find a new place to stay. Mabel felt worried again. Where could they go now?

Mabel wanted to go back to her old house. Her family said they couldn't go back to the old house because it wasn't the same anymore. The fire changed it so much that it wasn't safe to live in. Mabel felt *sad* and *angry*.

Mabel's family had to find somewhere to stay that was far away from the fire.

The family decided to stay in a place called a "shelter". It looked like a school with many beds inside.

When it was time to go to bed Mabel's tummy hurt. She couldn't sleep in the new bed... she felt **sick** and **nervous**.

At the shelter Mabel and her boy met many very nice people. Lots of people seemed very upset that they could not go home, but Mabel's family told her it would all be **okay**.

After many days and many nights at the shelter, Mabel's family got some **exciting** news. They were going to be able to move into a new apartment!

It wasn't as big as their old house...

It didn't have as many toys as the old house...

but it had a nice room just for Mabel and her boy to feel cozy and safe.

So even though things weren't exactly the same anymore, Mabel was still a very **happy** dog. She had a nice home, a boy who **loved** her, and her favorite chew toy that she played with every day.

About the Author:

Alison Hinson is a child and family therapist who has specialized in working with children who have experienced trauma or early childhood adversities for over 10 years. She is the author of the Mabel Book Series, written to assist children process their experiences with natural disasters.

She lives in Oregon with her husband, three children, and their very silly and loveable dogs, Mabel and Zeus.

Zeus and Mabel

Made in United States
Orlando, FL
04 February 2025